THE DOG PATROL

OUR CANINE COMPANIONS
AND THE KIDS WHO PROTECT THEM

ROB LAIDLAW

pajamapress

THIS BOOK IS DEDICATED TO every person, young or old, who has adopted, fostered, or helped dogs in need. You have truly made a difference in their lives.

First published in Canada and the United States in 2020

Text copyright © 2020 Rob Laidlaw
This edition copyright © 2020 Pajama Press Inc.
This is a first edition.

10 9 8 7 6 5 4 3 2 1

The publisher gratefully acknowledges the support of the Canada Council for the Arts and the Ontario Arts Council for its publishing program. We acknowledge the financial support of the Government of Canada through the Canada Book Fund (CBF) for our publishing activities.

Library and Archives Canada Cataloguing in Publication

Title: The dog patrol : our canine companions and the kids who protect them / Rob Laidlaw.
Names: Laidlaw, Rob, 1959- author.
Description: Includes index.
Identifiers: Canadiana 20190158468 | ISBN 9781772781038 (hardcover)
Subjects: LCSH: Dogs—Juvenile literature. | LCSH: Human-animal relationships—Juvenile literature. |
  LCSH: Children and animals—Juvenile literature. | LCSH: Animal welfare—Juvenile literature.
Classification: LCC SF426.5 .L35 2020 | DDC j636.7—dc23

Publisher Cataloging-in-Publication Data (U.S.)

Names: Laidlaw, Rob, author.
Title: The Dog Patrol : Our Canine Companions and the Kids Who Protect Them / Rob Laidlaw.
Description: Toronto, Ontario Canada : Pajama Press, 2019. | Includes index. | Summary: "Biologist and animal rights activist Rob Laidlaw explains dog biology, evolution, and behavior, and explores the dynamic relationship between humans and companion dogs. Amongst sections on dog care, training, and issues related to dog ownership are spotlight features on kids helping dogs. The book includes photographs, sidebars, a glossary, an index, and a dog anatomy gatefold"— Provided by publisher.
Identifiers: ISBN 978-1-77278-103-8 (hardcover)
Subjects: LCSH: Dogs -- Juvenile literature. | Dogs -- Behavior – Juvenile literature. | Dogs – Training – Juvenile literature. |
BISAC: JUVENILE NONFICTION / Animals / Dogs. | JUVENILE NONFICTION / Animals / Pets. | JUVENILE NONFICTION / Biography & Autobiography / Social Activists.
Classification: LCC SF426.5L35 |DDC 636.7 – dc23

Cover Image: White dog getting a bath–Shutterstock/©Lapina
Gatefold Image: White Jack Russell Terrier dog jumps in the summer-Shutterstock/©OlesyaNickolaeva
Cover and book design—Rebecca Bender

Manufactured by Qualibre Inc./Print Plus
Printed in China

Pajama Press Inc.
181 Carlaw Ave. Suite 251 Toronto, Ontario Canada, M4M 2S1

Distributed in Canada by UTP Distribution
5201 Dufferin Street Toronto, Ontario Canada, M3H 5T8

Distributed in the U.S. by Ingram Publisher Services
1 Ingram Blvd. La Vergne, TN 37086, USA

CONTENTS

A DOG NAMED KEEPER

When I was an inspector for the Toronto Humane Society, I received a call about a dog tied to a bulldozer in the west of the city. At night it was a deserted location of factories, warehouses, and open fields. I couldn't find the dog, so I went back the next day. Finally, I found the bulldozer the caller had described.

I saw a chain with one end fastened to the machine while the other snaked underneath. I knelt down and peered under, and I could see a short little tail wagging. I started to talk in a soft, friendly voice, and the dog looked at me. After a few minutes, she belly-crawled toward me, not quite sure whether to be happy or afraid, until I could reach out and touch her. Then she rolled over on her side, stubby tail wagging, and let me rub her tummy. She was a Kerry Blue Terrier.

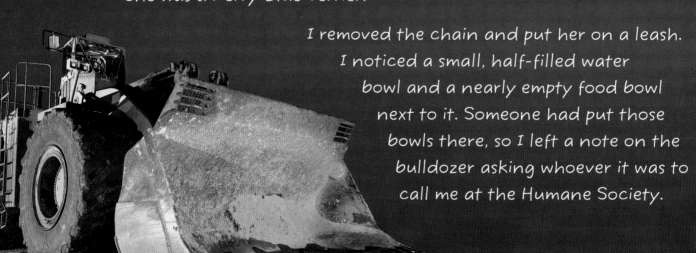

I removed the chain and put her on a leash. I noticed a small, half-filled water bowl and a nearly empty food bowl next to it. Someone had put those bowls there, so I left a note on the bulldozer asking whoever it was to call me at the Humane Society.

The next day I met with a man. He said he had rescued the dog. He seemed kind and had genuine affection for her, but he didn't seem to realize that living on a chain without proper attention just wasn't a good life. And he hadn't considered what it would be like when the cold of winter came. He agreed to give her up for adoption, and that's how I came to have one of the nicest dogs I've ever met.

I thought she was a keeper, so that's what I named her. Keeper became a friend to the other dogs in my house—Emmy, Mia, Bruiser, and Sam—and a foster mom to a litter of kittens. She lived to the ripe, old age of eighteen and a half years.

My experience in rescuing Keeper made me realize that many people, even when they love dogs, often don't understand dogs or realize what they need. They still think that providing food, water, and shelter is good enough, but it's not. And there are still many myths, mysteries, and misconceptions about dogs. This is why I've written this book, to encourage all of us to think a little bit more about our canine companions and what they need so we can make their lives as enriching and enjoyable as possible.

INTRODUCTION

Throughout my years as a professional animal protection advocate, I've had an opportunity to see how dogs live around the world. It's clear that dogs—especially those that don't live with human guardians—face a lot of major challenges, as I discussed in my book *No Shelter Here: Making the World a Kinder Place for Dogs*. In *The Dog Patrol* I focus more on our own companion dogs, highlighting some of the issues they face and discussing how they should be treated and cared for. I also want to tell you about some of the great ways dogs' lives are improving.

Companion dogs don't usually have the freedom to do normal dog things or to live according to the adaptations they've evolved. What they do, when they eat, who they associate with, where they sleep, how often they go out to relieve themselves, and the amount of time they spend alone are controlled by us.

We should be doing everything we can to understand the needs of dogs and to improve their lives. To inspire you, I include profiles in this book of young people who are doing just that. I call them members of the Dog Patrol, and their actions—whether simple or ambitious—are all meaningful to improving the lives of dogs.

I believe dogs should be treated with kindness, respect, and compassion. So please read on, get informed, get inspired, and get active! Pledge to make a difference in the lives of dogs, including your own canine companions.

—Rob

Companion Dogs: Non-working canines that typically live with and are cared for by human guardians

THE LONG HISTORY OF DOGS AND HUMANS

WHERE DID DOGS COME FROM?

Gray wolves are the ancestors of today's modern domesticated dogs. Between 40,000 and 20,000 years ago, it is thought that wolves established relationships with humans. Perhaps they followed groups of people to scavenge on the scraps of food they left behind. It's also possible that people captured young pups from their wild mothers and raised them by hand. The dogs may have become useful to humans as guards, protectors, or even an occasional food source. This relationship started the process of domestication, which resulted in the wolves becoming domesticated dogs.

Domesticated dogs were long thought to have come from the Middle East, but some evidence suggests they also may have emerged in China or Europe. Wherever they came from, we know that dogs and humans have had a long relationship. Prehistoric dog skulls were found in a European cave used by humans nearly 33,000 years ago. The earliest known burial site for both human and dog bones is in Germany, and it dates back more than 14,000 years. In the United States, a dog burial took place in Danger Cave, Utah about 11,000 years ago.

ALL 500–700 million domesticated dogs, from the tiny Chihuahua to the giant English Mastiff, are a single species. They may be called *Canis familiaris*, a species name. However, because they are less than 1% genetically different from wolves (*Canis lupus*), dogs are also sometimes called *Canis lupus familiaris*, a sub-species name.

Gray wolf, *Canis lupus*

HOW MANY official dog breeds are there? As of early 2019, the American Kennel Club recognizes 202 dog breeds, the UK's Kennel Club recognizes 211, and the Fédération Cynologique Internationale (World Canine Association) recognizes 344.

The Akita is an ancient breed

THE MORE ancient dog breeds include the Siberian Husky, Akita, Basenji, Chow Chow, and the Chinese Shar-Pei. Some modern breeds are collies, sheepdogs, and the hounds, many of them bred for specific work purposes, such as herding and hunting.

THE TRANSFORMATION OF DOGS

Wolves are adapted to chasing and catching their prey. They have an excellent sense of smell, eyesight that allows them to follow moving prey and see in low-light conditions, and exceptional hearing. They have large lungs and streamlined bodies with long legs for running great distances. With the use of their strong jaws and sharp teeth, wolves can grab, hold, and tear their prey.

While dogs were becoming domesticated, their wolf-like features altered. They developed smaller skulls, wider and shorter snouts, smaller jaws and teeth, and weaker bite strength. Unlike wolves, they also began to keep some of their puppy-like social behaviors as they grew into adults. And when humans started selectively breeding dogs, they created a wide diversity of modern breeds that bear little resemblance to wolves.

EARLY DOGS

Australian Dingo

Australia's Dingo is a descendent of dogs that may have come from southern China many thousands of years ago. The New Guinea Singing Dog is a primitive dog, similar to its wild ancestors, that humans brought to the island of New Guinea thousands of years ago. Other ancient dogs include North America's Carolina Dog, Israel's Canaan Dog, and the Pariah Dog of India, which is classified as a pure breed with a lineage dating back thousands of years.

New breeds are developed when a group of founder dogs with similar genetic and physical characteristics are isolated from other kinds of dogs and bred together. Unfortunately, this breeding of closely related dogs can result in disease-causing genes and other physical and mental health problems in the new breed. This phenomenon is called inbreeding depression. Mixed-breed dogs, often called mutts, are less likely to suffer from these conditions.

TOO SHORT, TOO LONG

Pugs, Bulldogs, and other breeds have been bred to have abnormally short heads, short noses, and flat faces. They are called *brachycephalic* dogs. They may have narrow, pinched nostrils, underdeveloped windpipes, and other physical issues that make it difficult for them to breathe or eat, causing gagging, choking, and vomiting. They can also quickly overheat in stressful or hot conditions. Short-faced dogs may also have bulgy eyes with eyelids that don't properly cover the eyes, repeated skin infections in the folds of skin on their faces, crowded teeth, and dental disease. Many veterinarians say they shouldn't be bred that way. Long-faced or *dolichocephalic* dogs, like German Shepherds, collies and greyhounds, pose fewer health concerns, but may experience fungal infections and nose tumors because of their longer faces and noses.

Bulldogs often have breathing problems

DOMESTICATING RUSSIAN FOXES

In 1959, Russian scientist Dimitry Belyaev tried to create domesticated foxes. From his founder population, he bred only the foxes that were the most tolerant of people. In each new generation, he followed the same process. In just a few generations, some foxes started to wag their tails, whimper, lick hands, and seek human attention like domesticated dogs. By the thirtieth generation, the foxes had major changes in their appearance, including floppy ears, shorter and curlier tails, and changes to the shape of their skulls, to their fur color, and even to their body chemistry. The rapid speed of these changes made scientists rethink how quickly wolves might have changed into dogs.

THE WORLD IS FULL OF DOGS

Dogs are among the world's most successful mammals with estimates placing the world dog population number at about 500–700 million. The United States has 75 million dogs, while Brazil has about 30 million, and China 23 million. Russia has about 15 million dogs, Japan 13 million, and the United Kingdom has about 8 million. Canada has approximately 7.9 million dogs.

COMPANION DOGS

The majority of dogs in North America, Europe, Australia, and Japan are companion dogs that live most or all of the time with people. Most dogs in the rest of the world are free-ranging, meaning they move about freely and are not under the control of people, although they may depend on humans for food.

Companion dogs (including working dogs) tend to come from humane society shelters, pounds, or rescues, pet stores, dog breeders (including puppy mills), from people who have allowed their own dogs to breed, or from purchases made online or through newspaper ads. In the United States in 2006, 15% of people acquired dogs from pet stores, 29% from breeders, and the rest from other sources.

PAWSITIVELY PAWSITIVE

An IKEA store in Italy opened its doors to stray dogs needing shelter. The store staff also provides food and water to the dogs. Hundreds of customers have thanked the store for helping the dogs, and millions of people have seen photos of them on social media.

According to a survey conducted by the American Pet Products Association in 2018, 60.2 million American households include a dog

THE DOG PATROL: SLED DOG ANTI-CRUELTY CRUSADER CAMERON BITOVE

Cameron Bitove

Cameron has always wanted to make the world a better place for people, animals, and the environment. In 2018, after watching the feature documentary *Sled Dogs*, eleven-year-old Cameron decided to do her school speech on the subject. She did a lot of research about commercial sled dog operations for tourists that chain their dogs for long periods. She even held a two-hour meeting with *Sled Dogs* director Fern Levitt. Not only did Cameron write her speech, she also became an advocate for the dogs used in sledding. She was invited to speak at the K-9 Unchain Canada "Break the Chains" rally, which occurred at the Ontario Legislative Building in Toronto on February 24, 2018. She also met with all the heads at her school to educate and challenge them on their extracurricular activity of dog sledding. When they said they wanted to do it anyway, she started a petition involving students from grades two to six and enlisted the help of Fern Levitt. Dog sledding was removed as a school activity for the 2018/19 season. Cameron now wants to end extracurricular commercial dog sledding excursions by private schools in Ontario and in other parts of Canada.

PAWSITIVELY PAWSITIVE

In 2018, the City of Montreal announced a new animal bylaw that will end the city's controversial ban on certain breeds of dogs. Instead, if a dog bites or attacks someone, that individual dog will be deemed *at risk*, will be required to undergo an expert evaluation, and may then be subject to a set of rules. The new bylaw is meant to ensure the safety of the public but keep Montreal an animal-friendly city.

THE DOG PATROL: ALL-AROUND DOG CHAMPION WILLOW PHELPS

From early on, Willow was nurtured and watched over by Zoe, her family's remarkable canine companion, so it is no surprise that she has grown up with a strong instinct to nurture and help dogs in return. In her 11 years, Willow has initiated many fundraisers to benefit animal charities, including sewing and selling dog and cat toys, running 5Ks, and swimming a one-mile lake. By 2019 she had raised nearly $15,000. Willow also teaches children how they can help foster dogs and puppies at shelters in New Jersey. In addition to offering volunteer foster care for puppies, Willow and her family also offer hospice care for chronically ill or elderly senior dogs and cats, giving them the comforts of home for the time they have left. She also volunteers regularly at Southern Paws, a local New Jersey rescue group. Her duties are to clean kennels, feed and groom puppies, and help socialize them until they go to their new homes. Her compassion and her efforts to improve the lives of animals has attracted a lot of attention and has resulted in her being awarded the title ASPCA Kid of the Year, a national honor, in 2016.

Willow Phelps

AMAZING CANINES!

Dogs are astonishing animals. Even though humans have lived with them for thousands of years, we keep learning new things about how their bodies work, how they live their lives, and how they think.

THE NOSE KNOWS

Smell is the most important sense to a dog. It's a big part of how they interpret the world. A dog's sense of smell is thousands of times more sensitive than that of any human. While we have about 5 million scent receptors, dogs have between 125 and 300 million. Dogs smell by breathing in airborne scent particles through their nostrils. These particles are absorbed by scent receptors in a thin layer of mucous inside the nose. Signals are then sent to the olfactory (scent-related) part of the dog's brain, an area that is proportionately 40 times larger than it is in a human brain. Additional particles can be transferred by a dog's tongue, from their sticky wet nose, to a special scent gland, called the *Jacobson's Organ*, located on the roof of the mouth. Their fantastic sense of smell is why dogs love to sniff so much.

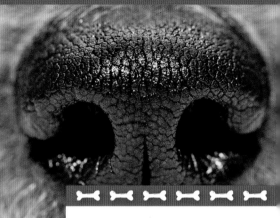

SMELLING CANCER

Dogs can be trained to detect almost anything by smell. They can find people buried in avalanches and recover human bodies. They can detect drugs, explosives, termites, and products made from endangered species. Medical dogs are even used to detect cancer. In a study conducted by the Medical Detection Dogs charity, specially trained dogs could detect prostate cancer in human urine 93% of the time. Other trained dogs could detect bladder, skin, lung, bowel, and other cancers. It's thought that the dogs are smelling waste products created by the cancer cells. Sniffing out cancer is a tremendous ability, but dogs are unlikely to replace other kinds of cancer screening because training is expensive and takes about six months. Plus, individual dogs probably couldn't screen hundreds or thousands of samples—they'd get bored.

WHY DO DOGS EAT POOP AND ROLL IN DEAD THINGS?

Yuck! A lot of dogs eat feces (poop), a behavior called *copraphagia*. No one really knows why they do it. It doesn't seem to matter if a dog is male or female, lives alone or with another dog, is old or young, or is well fed or not. One study suggests that 16% of dogs eat poop regularly, and up to 23% of the dogs studied had been observed doing it at least once. Since most dogs only eat fresh poop, one theory is that poop-eating is a holdover behavior from wolves, done perhaps to reduce the number of parasites around their dens, making it safer for their pups.

Many dogs also roll in feces or other smelly things, like dead animals. They may be trying to mask their own scent for hunting purposes, trying to smell more like an animal that might hunt them (a form of smelly camouflage), or trying to share their own scent while picking up that of others.

LISTENING AND SEEING

Dogs hear a broad range of sounds, including high frequency sounds that humans can't hear. For wolves surviving as predators, it makes a lot of sense—some of their prey might make high pitched sounds, so they need to hear them if they want to eat.

Dogs also have good eyesight, something a predator needs to survive, especially if they have to chase down their prey. Their night vision is excellent as well—their eyes have large pupils, corneas, and lenses; therefore, they collect lots of light. They also have a layer of tissue (called the *tapetum lucidum*) that reflects light back through the retina (the part of the eye that receives light), giving it a second chance to be picked up by the eye's photoreceptors. This layer is why a dog's eyes seem to glow in the dark. In Malaysia I encountered a dog navigating in a cave with almost no light. I couldn't see, but the dog could.

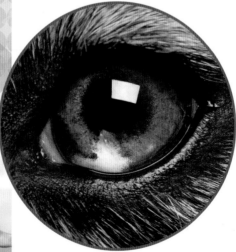

(Above) Dogs have two color receptors in their eyes, while humans have three. They can see yellows, blues, and shades of gray

(Right) Erect ears, which many modern dogs don't have, can be directed toward a sound to make it easier to hear.

Because dogs of different ages have different nutritional needs, dog food companies sell products for puppies, adults, and seniors

Some foods, including chocolate, coffee, grapes, onions, garlic, and avocados, can be toxic to dogs

DOGGIE DIGESTION

Are dogs pure carnivores, like their wolf ancestors, or are they scavengers that can eat a wider variety of food? Recent research shows that dogs are genetically different from wolves in ways that give them a greater ability to process starches (carbohydrates) than wolves can. Dogs are omnivorous and that's why millions of them around the world can live on largely vegetarian diets. But no matter what diet a dog has, it's important to make sure it meets all of their nutritional needs.

GETTING NECESSARY NUTRITION

All dogs require a number of basic nutrients in order to maintain good health. They are protein, carbohydrates, fats, vitamins, minerals, and water. Nutrients are needed for keeping every part of the dog's body, including their brain, healthy and working. There are all kinds of diets promoted for dogs, but a simple rule is to look for food that is well balanced with real, whole ingredients that is low in calories.

SENSING SEIZURES

Seizure alert dogs seem able to predict epileptic seizures. We don't know how they do it, but scientists are studying this amazing ability. Perhaps the dogs are picking up very subtle physical cues, such as odors generated by people about to have a seizure, or changes in their behavior that we don't notice.

West Highland White Terriers were used to hunt rodents on farms

Service dogs wear vests to show they are working

HOW SMART ARE DOGS?

Dogs can communicate and cooperate with other dogs and humans, learn from each other, solve problems, remember where things are and how to navigate their territory, learn to understand up to 250 words, count to 4 or 5, and much more. All dogs have a fairly large brain that weighs approximately 1/125th of their total weight (human brains are 1/50th of our total weight). Some experts say the intelligence of an average dog is about the same as that of a 2-year-old child.

According to renowned dog scientist Dr. Stanley Coren, there are three components of dog intelligence:

1. Instinctive intelligence—the ability to perform the tasks it was bred for, such as fetching, stalking, herding, patrolling, guarding, or being a companion

2. Adaptive intelligence—the ability to solve problems

3. Working and obedience intelligence— the ability to learn from humans

Border Collies, thought to be the world's smartest dogs, are often trained to herd sheep

DOG TALK

Dogs have complex ways of communicating and use a variety of sounds, body signals, and chemical cues to convey information. Barking is the most familiar sound dogs make, but others are growls, whines, yelps, whimpers, and howls. They also communicate through body signals, including stance, tail position, hair raising, ear turning, and lip curling. The most obvious body signal, that almost everyone knows, is tail wagging. What the tail wagging means can depend on the kind of dog, the position of the tail, and how it is wagged. It can express positive emotions, but it can also mean a dog is fearful or insecure. It may even be a warning that a dog may bite.

Barking is a normal type dog of communication, but it's also one of the most commonly cited dog behavior problems. There's no one reason to explain why some dogs bark all the time. They may be experiencing fear, alarm, boredom, loneliness, or anxiety, or they may think they are defending their territory.

This dog's posture and wagging tail express happiness

NEVER SHOUT at a dog to make them stop barking as that can actually make them bark more. Instead, try to identify the cause of the barking and then use training or behavior modification to address it. If you need help, call your local humane society, animal rescue, or dog protection group, and ask if they can connect you to a dog behaviorist.

This dog is using body language to show anxiety

Barking is a normal dog reaction to many things

SEPARATION ANXIETY

Many dogs become upset when they are left alone, especially if they lack mental stimulation or exercise. Dogs may show this separation anxiety by barking, chewing, trying to escape, pooping in the house, pacing, or even self-mutilating (chewing on their own bodies, legs, or tails).

Luckily, there are methods that can help desensitize dogs to being alone. Starting with very short periods of time, such as a minute or two, a dog's time alone can gradually be increased. It helps the dog learn that they are not being abandoned and that they don't need to panic.

Other ways of helping dogs cope include visiting your dog during the day, getting a family member or friend to drop in, hiring a dog walker, finding a doggie daycare facility, or even taking your dog to school or work.

THE SOCIAL NEEDS OF DOGS

Since dogs evolved from highly social wolves that live in families or packs, it's no surprise that dogs are exceptionally social animals. However, the majority of dogs kept as companions are single dogs who live with their human guardians, either indoors or confined to a yard. They are often left alone from morning until late afternoon or early evening, sometimes ten or twelve hours per day. That's way too long to leave a dog alone. They need to get out to relieve themselves every four to six hours, stretch their legs, exercise, and to alleviate boredom. Even four hours is too long for senior dogs and, ideally, puppies shouldn't be left alone at all.

Dogs experience many of the same emotions that people do. They can be happy, joyful, and excited, but they can also be anxious, fearful, lonely and depressed. In fact, veterinarians often prescribe the same anti-depression drugs that people use to help address dog depression and other emotional issues. Dogs are meant to be physically and mentally active, and they are meant to socialize during the day. When they're regularly left alone in a house, they suffer for it.

Crating dogs to stop them from damaging the home can make separation anxiety worse

THE DOG PATROL: SENIOR-DOG SPECIALIST ANALEIGH PAINTER

Even though Analeigh is only eight years old, this Edmonton, Alberta, resident helps dogs from ARTS Senior Animal Rescue on a daily basis. She cares for these foster dogs in her home where she feeds, grooms, administers medications, cleans up, and does all of the other tasks required to take care of the dogs. Perhaps most importantly, she cuddles and plays with them, showing each dog that that they are safe and can be calm, relaxed, and unafraid. Analeigh also participates in awareness events where she talks to the public, answers their questions, helps to handle dogs and cats when their fosters are not present, cleans up when there are accidents, and performs many other tasks. These events can be six hours or longer, but Analeigh stays and makes sure the animals all have what they need. She also helps manage pet supplies and food collected by her family for dogs in need. Analeigh organizes and packs them away, and checks expiration dates. And, of course, Analeigh also looks after her own three dogs. Two of them are dogs with high needs that were rescued as seniors, but Analeigh diligently cares for them and assists in their recovery. In her spare time, she also advocates for better treatment for wild animals in captivity.

Analeigh Painter

Sam (left) and Ella Seeley (above)

THE DOG PATROL: COMFORT AND CARE PROVIDER ELLA SEELEY

Sam came into twelve-year-old Ella Seeley's life shortly after he had arrived at neighbor Vera's house. Rescued from the streets of Egypt, Sam was a skinny, blind Egyptian Baladi Dog, an ancient breed. He had been beaten and was not used to human touch. Being blind, he had to learn to cope with his new surroundings, and he also had to struggle through many seizures. Ella helped Vera rehabilitate Sam by walking and interacting with him, often twice a day. She taught him to sit, to relax, and to not be afraid of others. It took many months for Ella to be able to rub his belly and for Sam to be able to comfortably go up and down steps. He became a very smart, strong, kind, and friendly dog, making everyone he met smile. After many adoption meetings and visits, a man named Tim adopted Sam. He lived a joyful, full life, until a major seizure ended it abruptly. That was sad news for Ella to hear. Sam had been her partner for a long time, but she knew she had made his life better by training, comforting, and helping him. Ella has many fond memories of Sam and she wants everyone to know that small actions can make a big difference to the lives of dogs.

PAWSITIVELY PAWSITIVE

Some companies give their staff paid time off when they acquire a puppy, so they can bond with the pup and help them settle into their new home. At HarperCollins in India, they see this as a way of promoting pet adoptions. Some companies also provide time off when a pet passes away.

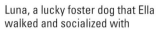

Luna, a lucky foster dog that Ella walked and socialized with

SO YOU WANT A DOG?

There are many ways to get a dog and some are more responsible than others. Make sure you are informed about the source of your dog, so that you are not supporting businesses that exploit dogs for profit.

PUPPY MILL PUPPIES

A puppy mill is a business that mass produces puppies as cheaply as possible for the pet trade. Dogs in puppy mills may be kept in crowded, dirty cages in dim sheds and barns with poor food and little or no veterinary care. Many become sick or injured in these miserable conditions.

Puppy mills sell their puppies through pet stores and through advertisements in newspapers or online. The best way to fight them is to not buy from those sources.

THERE COULD BE up to 10,000 puppy mills in the United States, and 2,000 or more in Canada, collectively producing more than 2 million puppies every year. In most areas they are not illegal.

PAWSITIVELY PAWSITIVE

To fight puppy mills, a growing number of towns and cities have banned the sale of live cats and dogs in pet stores unless they are from rescue centers. On January 1, 2019, California became the first state to pass such a law. Some pet stores, including entire chains, have become satellite adoption centers for shelter and rescue dogs.

21

Austin and Maya

Austin and Frannie

THE DOG PATROL: AUSTIN DELOS SANTOS, MAKING A DIFFERENCE FOR DOGS

During his high school sophomore year, Austin Delos Santos started volunteering at Best Friends Pet Adoption and Spay/Neuter Center in Los Angeles. He initially worked with the easygoing dogs, but it wasn't long before he began dealing with the more excitable, nervous, or fearful dogs that came in, helping them gain confidence and preparing them for adoption. In addition to volunteering at the Center, Austin was also an organizer of his high school's animal care club where he conducted programs to collect supplies like blankets, toys, dog beds, and food for the Center. The group also encouraged other kids to get involved and raised much-needed awareness about spaying and neutering, puppy mills, and other dog issues. One of Austin's most important tasks was mentoring new volunteers at the Center, and he conducted both group and individual mentorship sessions, hoping to inspire volunteers to make a commitment and return to help the dogs. Austin is now in university and hopes to become a registered nurse, but no doubt he will always be an advocate for dogs and other animals.

Austin and Coco

DOG BREEDING

If you choose to buy a dog from a breeder, look for these signs that they are a responsible one:

- They specialize in only one or two breeds.

- They are members of the breed club or association.

- They ask questions about you.

- They ask you to sign an application or contract.

- The parent dogs and puppies live in a clean, comfortable space with proper shelter and room to play.

- The dogs look healthy and can socialize with each other.

A breeder should never let puppies younger than eight weeks leave their mother

If you see poor conditions at a breeder, register a complaint with the local humane society or municipal authority. To find a more responsible breeder, get advice from a breed club or association, humane society, dog rescue group, or animal welfare organization that deals with dog issues.

IN COUNTRIES with large numbers of free-roaming dogs, there are also Catch & Release shelters that take in street dogs, spay or neuter them so they will not have puppies, treat injuries and illnesses, and then release them back into the streets. This is a cruelty-free way to help control the number of dogs.

ADOPT A DOG, SAVE A LIFE!

If you adopt a dog from a shelter, pound or rescue, you may be saving the life of a dog who would otherwise be destroyed. If you're looking for a specific breed, remember that nearly one third of shelter dogs are purebred and many dog rescue groups focus on specific breeds. Petfinder.com is the world's largest online database of animals needing a home and a great place to find a dog. They're linked to shelters and have tens of thousands of adoptable dogs of all breeds on their website.

SHELTERS AND POUNDS

Most shelters can be lumped into one of two categories:

1. Open Admission Shelters accept whatever dogs are brought to them and, under certain circumstances, will euthanize (put down) dogs.

2. No-Kill Shelters take in dogs but don't put them down unless they have untreatable injuries or incurable illnesses, or are too dangerous to adopt out.

Sadly, more than 1.2 million dogs are still destroyed in North American shelters every year, but steps are being taken to greatly reduce that number. Many Open Admission shelters are now delivering all kinds of programs that promote dog adoptions, including partnering with dog rescue groups, making shelters better for the dogs, and making them more inviting to the public.

THE DOG PATROL: PREMIER FOREVER HOME FINDER AVA CALISE

After having spent nearly all of her life with rescue dogs brought home by her mother, Ava Calise understood early on how badly treated so many of them were. She decided to take action to help. Ava spends most of her free time volunteering for several animal rescue groups. Waking at 6:00 a.m., she cares for fostered dogs (specializing in dogs that are extremely stressed or sick), uses social media to find them forever homes, or assists with their transport from Oklahoma City (OKC) to New York and New Jersey to be adopted. She happily says she has been able to save more lives than she can count. A long, white Dachshund mix named Coco, rescued from a hoarding case in OKC, was a special case for Ava. In transport Coco was terrified. Ava patiently cared for him for many months afterward, moving slowly and providing gentle leadership. Finally, Ava gained his trust and the love that makes Coco so special to her. Ava was sad to see him go to his forever home but knew it was for the best because she could now assist another dog in need. Ava enjoys every little thing about caring for dogs, from feeding to cleaning cages to giving them comfort. She says that as long as the dogs end up happy, so is she.

PAWSITIVELY PAWSITIVE

After posting a video on Facebook requesting comfy armchairs for their dogs, the Knox County Humane Society in Illinois was overwhelmed with responses. Now every dog can curl up on a comfortable, soft chair for as long as they are at the shelter.

Ava Calise

Dogs at this facility enjoy interaction and training on an agility course

WHAT MAKES A GOOD SHELTER?

Here's a list of some of the things that good shelters do:

☻ Make the physical, psychological, and behavioral needs of dogs their highest priority

☻ Allow dogs to be dogs by giving them opportunities to socialize and play (or do their best to accomplish that by providing walks, exercise, and other enrichment)

☻ Spay or neuter all animals before they are adopted

☻ Provide all animals with a full veterinary examination, vaccinations, and whatever other medical care is necessary

☻ Carefully screen all potential adopters through an application and interview process

☻ Conduct temperament tests to predict how a dog will behave toward humans and other dogs (recognizing they may not always be 100% accurate)

☻ Provide ongoing support and advice to adopters

Good rescues take care of dogs' health needs

ANIMAL RESCUE

SELL
R

e first bred in England
rgetic dogs that love to

IFLE joint is similar
's knee

The **WITHERS** is the bony high between a dog's shoulder blades

- Conduct programs that reach out to the community, promote adoptions, and bring dogs to the people

- Stay open when people are available, such as nights and weekends

- Make shelters friendly, welcoming places

- Cooperate with other dog rescue and welfare organizations

- Make all efforts possible to drastically reduce the numbers of dogs killed

- Actively support changes in laws and other measures that protect dogs

DOG RESCUE LIFELINE

Thousands of dog rescues help abandoned, surrendered, seized, or neglected dogs from the streets, in remote areas, such as isolated northern communities, or even overseas. Many relocate dogs back to North America or Europe. Some rescues have their own shelters, but many send dogs to be fostered in the homes of dedicated volunteers. Increasingly, rescues are cooperating with humane society shelters and pounds. One of their important initiatives is moving dogs from areas where shelters and rescues are overpopulated to shelters in other areas that don't have enough dogs to meet the adoption demand.

THE DOG PATROL: RESCUE DOG HERO CAROLINE CAPUZZI

After her beloved German Shepherd, Zoey, passed away in 2016, high school student Caroline Capuzzi decided to do something to highlight the plight of rescue dogs. She started working at the West Chester Animal Hospital kennel in the late spring of 2017, the same year she adopted Stella, a Border Collie mix. She fed the dogs, cleaned their kennels, and took them for walks. Many of the dogs boarded at the facility were rescues, so she learned about their tragic pasts and how they needed help. After consulting with her dad, Caroline decided to write a book that could be used to raise awareness about rescue dogs, promote their adoption, and raise funds for dog rescue organizations. She soon assembled twenty-five stories and published them in a book titled *Dog Joy: Amazing Stories of the Indescribable Love Only a Rescued Dog Can Give*. Each dog story also highlights a dog rescue, shelter, or group. As I wrote this section, more than $5000 worth of books had been sold, and Caroline had also donated $1100 worth of books to dog rescues. Caroline is now promoting *Dog Joy* books to other shelters and rescues in the hope that they'll take advantage of this unique initiative for helping dogs by pulling together a book of their own rescue stories.

Caroline Capuzzi

ADOPTING A DOG: DO YOUR HOMEWORK

Before you get a dog, there are some important questions to ask. Can you meet a dog's needs? Do all your family members want a dog? Will it be left alone very much? Can you afford vaccinations and veterinary bills?

Reading books, searching the internet, and talking to shelter and animal welfare workers can give you valuable information about specific breeds, their behaviors, their personality traits, and how much exercise they need. Veterinarians can tell you about possible health problems associated with certain breeds.

The information you collect might convince you not to get a dog, but that's okay. If you can't meet a dog's needs, it's probably best to wait.

CHOOSE THE DOG THAT'S RIGHT FOR YOU

Border Collies, Jack Russell Terriers, and Siberian Huskies are high-energy dogs that may not be a good fit for someone who doesn't go out much. If you want a dog to go running with you every day, you might not want a Bulldog or a Bassett Hound. If you live in a small apartment, you probably don't want to adopt a large dog like a Great Dane or a Saint Bernard. Your dog should match your lifestyle, energy level, and where you live.

You also have to think about whether you want an adult dog or a puppy, a short-haired breed or long-haired one.

BLACK DOG SYNDROME

Black dogs can be difficult to adopt out, a phenomenon called Black Dog Syndrome (BDS). No one knows why this happens. Maybe it's because black animals are often associated with evil in horror movies and television shows. If you plan to adopt a dog, keep BDS in mind. There are lots of wonderful black dogs that need homes.

PAWSITIVELY PAWSITIVE

Humane societies and shelters across Canada and the United States have established reading programs that pair shelter dogs with kids learning to read. It helps the dogs feel loved and gets them used to people, while helping the kids get better at reading.

WHAT ABOUT DOGS WITH SPECIAL NEEDS?

Dogs with special needs, whether blind, deaf, partially paralyzed, or missing a limb, need homes too. They may present unique challenges to their guardians, but they can still make great companions. Dogs with special needs can often run, jump, play, go for walks and hikes, and do most of the things that other dogs can. When adopting, don't dismiss these dogs. They need love and companionship too.

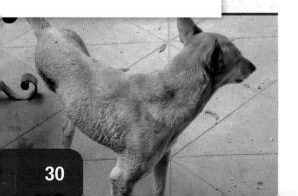

GET TO KNOW EACH OTHER

Before you adopt a dog, you and your family should spend at least a few hours with her. Many shelters have dog meet-and-greet rooms, and you may even be able to take the dog out for a walk. If you're adopting from someone who is giving up a pet dog, hang out with the dog in his house and yard, and ask lots of questions.

THE APPLICATION PROCESS

Most shelters require adopters to complete an application and interview. They'll want to know where the dog will live, who will take it for walks, if there are other animals in the house, and how long the dog will be left alone. They want to ensure that they don't adopt dogs out to homes where they won't be taken care of. The interviews are also a chance for you to ask your own questions.

Your application will be considered over the next day or so. If it is approved, you'll have to pay an adoption fee. The process is similar with legitimate rescue organizations.

PUREBRED PROBLEMS

Purebred dogs are expected to satisfy a breed standard, which is a set of required physical features established by their breed club or association. But the breeding of closely related dogs to achieve this can cause disease-causing genes and other problems to be passed

Breathing problems can affect Pugs (right) and Pekingese

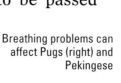

on at higher rates. That can mean increased chances of certain dog breeds having physical difficulties and inherited diseases. When adopting purebred dogs, be aware of what problems might surface later.

Great Danes often have skeletal problems

IN THE DOGHOUSE: COSMETIC SURGERIES

Cosmetic surgeries are done because owners want their dog to look a certain way (often set by a breed standard). Tail-docking is the removal of part of the tail through surgery or by constricting blood flow to the tail until it falls off. Ear cropping is when up to 2/3 of a dog's ear flap is removed so that it heals into a pointy position.

The Canadian Veterinary Medical Association (CVMA) and most animal welfare groups oppose cosmetic ear cropping and tail docking, and encourage breed clubs to change their standards to discourage these practices.

Cocker spaniels (below) and Rottweillers often have their tails docked.

The ears of Dobermans (right) and Boxers are often cropped

AUSTRALIA, New Zealand, South Africa and most European countries forbid tail docking, and many other jurisdictions restrict the practice. Ear cropping is banned in many jurisdictions, such as the Canadian provinces of New Brunswick, Nova Scotia, Prince Edward Island, Newfoundland, Manitoba, Saskatchewan, and British Columbia, as well as Australia, New Zealand and parts of Europe.

In February 2019, the Alberta Veterinary Medical Association voted to ban cosmetic surgeries on dogs and cats. The ban includes ear cropping, tail docking, declawing, cosmetic dentistry, body piercing, devocalization and several other procedures.

PAWSITIVELY PAWSITIVE

The La Vista police department is promoting dog adoptions through the innovative K9 Cop For a Day program. Once a month, an adoptable dog from the Nebraska Humane Society spends part of a day riding along with a police officer while they go about their duties in the community. It's a great way of raising awareness about dogs needing homes.

Ione Gibson

PRC members

THE IMPORTANCE OF SPAY AND NEUTER

Today in North America, millions of dogs are destroyed in shelters and pounds because no one comes to adopt them. By getting your dog spayed or neutered (sterilized), you'll be part of the solution to the overpopulation crisis.

Dogs are usually spayed or neutered at six to nine months old, but the procedures can also be done on older or younger dogs.

THE DOG PATROL: THE CITIZENS' PET RESPONSIBILITY COMMITTEE — FIGHTING PET OVERPOPULATION

More than a decade ago, several adults got together and formed The Citizens' Pet Responsibility Committee (PRC) of Moore County in North Carolina with a goal of combating pet overpopulation. They realized the important role that young people could play, so they developed a program aimed at fourth graders. It would educate them about being responsible pet owners and help decrease the number of pets entering the local shelter.

The program encourages acts of advocacy, big and small, to address neglect and abuse, and to be a positive force for animals. Ione Gibson from Pinehurst Elementary School baked cookies and made lemonade to sell, with proceeds going to the local county shelter. Students at the O'Neal School raised money for supplies for two puppies training as service dogs for veterans through the Continuing the Mission organization. Payton Caldwell from Vass-Lakeview

Students at the O'Neal School

Elementary School volunteers with the PRC at events, encouraging adults and students to make a difference for the pets in their community. By involving fourth graders in these initiatives and also in spreading the word about spaying and neutering, the PRC has reduced the number of pets entering the local shelter from more than 5,000 per year to just over 2,500.

THE DOG PATROL: ANIMAL WELFARE PROMOTER MANAHA NAKAKITA

Thirteen-year-old Manaha Nakakita lives in Kagawa Prefecture, Japan. Her dog Silver died when she was just nine years old, prompting Manaha to do some research about the lives of dogs and cats in her prefecture. She learned that between 2010 and 2018, Kagawa Prefecture destroyed more unwanted dogs than anywhere else in Japan. Manaha is a member of an organization that provides children with a place to gather and spend time together. In April 2017, she and her friends set up an animal welfare group called WanNyanPeaSmile. The group advocates for dogs and cats, and Manaha plans to produce a picture book encouraging people to understand the importance of animal welfare. At the time this book was written, she had already collected 1,000,000 Yen ($9,050 US) from more than 100 donors through crowdfunding for the project. Manaha's efforts have been recognized by other dog activists, celebrities, and politicians. She was even invited to read one of her essays to the Governor, Takamatsu City Mayor, and 400 people attending a Kagawa Prefecture 100th anniversary event organized by the Lion's Club.

Manaha Nakakita

PAWSITIVELY PAWSITIVE

In 2017, Taiwan became the first country in Asia to ban the consumption of dog and cat meat. Back in 1998, the country had made it illegal to raise, kill, and sell dogs and cats for human consumption.

GETTING ALONG WITH YOUR DOG

HOW TO PET YOUR OWN DOG

Not many people give much thought about how to pet their own dog. Here are a few tips to remember:

- Use slow, calm, relaxed motions when petting your dog and avoid jerky, fast motions.

- Avoid petting your dog's face or grabbing their muzzle;

- Don't hug or squeeze your dog as they may feel trapped;

- Don't reach over your dog's head to pet them as they can see that as threatening;

- If your dog doesn't want contact, leave them alone. Many dogs don't really like being touched.

REWARDS ARE BETTER THAN PUNISHMENT

In the past, many people thought dogs should be trained using punishment, also called negative reinforcement, to discourage unwanted behaviors. This training could include shouting, hitting, shocking, violently tugging the leash, or using a prong or shock collar. Increasingly, those actions are considered cruel and unhelpful because they can cause fear and pain, and may confuse a dog about how to behave. More humane, reward-based forms of dog training have become popular. In positive-reinforcement training, dogs are rewarded for good behavior with something positive, like praise, petting, a special toy, or a treat.

Scientists have studied whether punishment or reward is better for achieving dog training results. It turns out that reward-based techniques are not only kinder—they are more effective. Another benefit is that positive reinforcement doesn't make dogs more aggressive, which is a risk when using negative reinforcement.

Most companion dogs receive little, if any, professional training, but it is worth considering. It won't necessarily solve every behavior problem, but it can help reduce them and make them more manageable. That can often mean better treatment for dogs and a better life for both them and their human guardians.

PROTECT YOURSELF FROM DOG BITES

According to the American Veterinary Medical Association there are more than 4.5 million dog bites every year in the United States alone. In 2008, more than 300,000 hospital emergency department visits involved a dog bite. Kids are the most likely to be bitten, but there are ways to reduce the chance of a dog bite:

- Remember, all dogs can bite.

- Don't approach strange or unfamiliar dogs.

- If an unfamiliar dog comes near you, stay still until it goes away. Don't run or make noise.

- If you're on your bike, dismount, stay where you are, and position your bike between you and the dog.

- Don't try to pet a leashed dog without asking permission from its guardian. Always let the dog sniff you first.

- Don't look a dog in the eye. Some see it as a threat or challenge.

- Never approach a chained dog or a dog in a fenced yard.

- Never bother a dog that's eating, sleeping or tending puppies.

- Don't play aggressive games with dogs or encourage them to bite.

Chained dogs may feel the need to defend their territory

A dog who is disturbed while eating may feel threatened

Let strange dogs sniff your closed fist—a flat palm is easier to nip

35

st Friendly dog brown-white color. Responds to the name Jo
Finding a decent reward. Call 111-222-333

SUBSTANTIAL
REWARD

FINDING A LOST DOG

If your dog is lost, act fast and take the following steps:

- Stop what you're doing and start your search as soon as possible. The first 24 hours are often the most important. Get family and friends involved.

- Make a flier with a good photo of your dog, your phone number, and information about a reward, if you can afford to offer one.

- Make sure you or a family member are always reachable by phone. Once people know about your lost dog, they'll call if they have information. If you have to let calls go to your answering service, tell people you'll pick up messages frequently and ask them to leave their name and number.

- Post your fliers in places where lots of people will notice them, such as at community centers and schools, and especially at pet-related places like humane societies, animal control centers, veterinary offices, and dog parks. Other dog guardians are the most likely people to notice unattended or lost dogs.

- List your dog on Helping Lost Pets (www.helpinglostpets. com), FidoFinder (www.fidofinder.com) or other sites that list lost pets. Some of them send alerts out to subscribers in the area where a dog is lost. Also look for online lost/found pet listings and watch them every day.

- Create a list of all shelters, animal control centers and dog rescues in your region. Call or, better yet, visit them every day if you can. Don't assume they'll recognize your dog if they happen to be in their facilities. Make a similar list of all the veterinary clinics and call them regularly as well.

- Check out for-sale ads to see if someone is trying to sell your dog.

- Ask your local newspaper, radio, and television stations to announce that your dog is lost. Mention the reward or anything else that you think might grab their attention.

- Just because you've already looked in one area, don't assume your dog isn't there. You may not have seen them the first time around, or they may be on the move. Keep looking.

- Don't give up. You are your canine friend's best hope.

MICROCHIPS— A GREAT IDEA

Dogs should always be wearing identification tags, but they should also be microchipped as an added safeguard. Microchips are tiny glass-enclosed computer chips that are inserted into a dog's skin, usually between the shoulder blades. The content of a microchip can be read by veterinary or shelter staff with a scanner. The staff can then retrieve information about a dog's guardians and home. Microchips don't require a battery, they never wear out, and dogs don't feel them or even know they're there. They don't prevent dogs from getting lost, but they increase the chance of a dog making it home safe and sound.

CRATING ABUSE

A crate is a portable kennel made of metal or plastic. Many people confine puppies in crates for a short time for house training. But many adult dogs are confined in crates for extended periods of time, often every day and sometimes at night too, because they bark a lot or chew things.

Crating is convenient for dog guardians, but it deprives dogs of the freedom to stretch out, move around, and relieve themselves. It's also boring and can lead to behavior problems, such as excessive barking or aggression. Some experts suggest that the maximum time any dog should be confined is four hours (puppies less than one hour), but the less time a dog is crated the better. Excessive use of crates is abusive and cruel.

There are alternatives, such as providing an entire room in your home for your dog or installing a doggie door that allows them to go outside into an enclosed area. Having a family member, friend, or neighbor check on or look after your dog may also be an option. Some people are able to take their dog to work or use a doggie daycare service.

Before getting a dog, potential guardians should make sure they have alternatives to crating

PLEASE, NO MORE CHAINS

Chaining (or tethering) dogs alone for long periods of time is one of the worst dog abuses. The lives of chained dogs are often filled with frustration, boredom, and extreme loneliness. Their health and welfare can also be poor from lack of exercise and inappropriate shelter. For many dogs, these problems are made even worse by a lack of proper food and veterinary care.

Chained dogs may bark excessively because they can't engage in any normal dog activities, get virtually no exercise, and are lacking in love, companionship, and normal social interactions. Chaining can even make normally friendly dogs aggressive and dangerous. They may become protective or territorial and see anyone who comes too close, including children, as a threat. Studies show that chained dogs are far more likely to be biters and that most of the victims of chained dog attacks are children.

Several states and hundreds of North American towns and cities have laws that either ban chaining or limit how long dogs can be chained. The great news for chained dogs is that additional laws to get them off their chains are being considered and passed every year.

HOW TO KEEP YOUR DOG UN-CHAINED OR UN-TETHERED

- Bring your dog inside—Dogs need to be part of a pack or family. If your dog has too much energy, learn about humane training and how to help them change their behavior.

- Put up a fence—Fences allow more room for dogs to move around and exercise.

- Put up a trolley—A leash attached to an overhead cable can also give a dog an opportunity to run.

- Fix the fence you already have—If your dog can jump your fence, there are many ways of fixing it to prevent jumping. Planting bushes along the length of a fence will discourage dogs from getting a running start.

- Spay or neuter your dog—Sterilization can reduce your dog's desire to roam

- Go for walks—Walking will work off a dog's excess energy, making them even better behaved in your home. A tired dog is more likely to be a content dog.

An obvious sign of a chained dog is the circle of bare, hard-packed earth that extends only as far as the chain reaches. They have to eat, sleep, pee, and poop in that small area

HOW TO HELP CHAINED DOGS

- Ask an adult to talk to the dog's guardian.

- If the dog is sick, injured, or too thin, or if it is left outside in all weather, contact your local animal control or humane society.

- Keep watching the dog. If things don't get better, make another complaint.

- Offer to give the dog food, water, toys, or shelter—but don't approach a chained dog unless an adult you trust is present.

- Educate people about why chaining is cruel.

- Get an anti-chaining law passed in your community.

THE DOG PATROL: FOSTER FUNDING EXPERT GENEVIÈVE PLANTE

Since she was very young, Geneviève Plante has shared her house, in La Ronge, Saskatchewan, with foster dogs. She helps care for them, doing everything from changing bedding to bathing them and giving them lots of attention. She especially enjoys mother dogs with puppies. During the fall of 2017, Geneviève started to think she'd like to raise $1,000 for Northern Animal Rescue (NAR) at her next birthday party. The party raised about $150, so Geneviève set out to make up the rest. She managed to hold about 11 lemonade stands on the corner of her street before the end of August, raising an additional $750. With a few more donations, Geneviève soon surpassed her goal and reached a total of $1087.10. At one of NAR's own fundraising events, Geneviève presented an oversized cheque to the organization and she was generously given a sweater with the NAR logo and a large stuffed dog. A story with her picture even made it into the local paper.

Geneviève Plante

THE DOG PATROL: ACE ANIMAL ADVOCATE MOLLY MATLOW

At only six years old, Toronto, Canada, resident Molly Matlow is a powerful advocate for dogs and all other animals. Following in the footsteps of her mother, who works for a prominent animal protection organization, Molly misses no opportunity to let people know that dogs and other animals have feelings and needs, and that everyone should be kind, compassionate, and respectful to them. Molly used her birthday to raise funds for a local wildlife rescue center, instead of receiving gifts, and she plans to pick a different animal charity to support each year. She is also trying to educate her friends and classmates about all kinds of animal issues and is quite eloquent about why wild animals belong in the wild and shouldn't be caged or used for entertainment. She has spoken out against bringing wild animals into the classroom and discourages people from participating in wild animal photo sessions at popular holiday destinations. As soon as she is old enough, Molly plans to volunteer at a humane society where she'll have the chance to help dogs, cats, and other animals in need. In the meantime, Molly does whatever she can to help animals wherever she encounters them.

Molly Matlow

PAWSITIVELY PAWSITIVE

Shelters across the continent are running programs that pair shelter dogs with temporary foster homes during the Thanksgiving holiday. Not only does it give the dogs a break from being in the shelter all day long, many of the temporary foster homes have become their permanent homes.

A DOG'S LIFE AT HOME

DOG NEEDS

Good nutritious food, fresh water, and shelter are important to dogs, but they need much more than that to live happy, healthy lives.

🐾 **Friendship:** Dogs should be part of a family and not left alone all the time. Spend as much time as possible with your dog and their life will be much better.

🐾 **Things to do:** Regular, daily walks, runs, and play sessions help keep dogs healthy and prevent them from becoming bored, overweight, or aggressive. Throw a ball, go to the dog park, or hike a local trail. Your dog will love it and so will you.

🐾 **Tender loving care:** Cleaning, brushing, nail clipping, and other regular grooming tasks make companion dogs feel comfortable and healthy. Vaccinations prevent disease and trips to the veterinarian can identify issues before they become too serious.

RELAX THE LEASH

Walks are essential to dog health and welfare because they provide exercise, mental stimulation, and a break from routine dog life. Unfortunately, studies show that many dogs are hardly walked at all. In one study, 31% of dogs kept in yards were walked once a week or less, while another study found just 29% of guardians walked their dog once or twice a week. Dog walks are important. If someone doesn't want to walk their dog, they should think about whether they should have a dog at all.

It's important for dog guardians to remember whom the walk is for. It's for your dog, so walks shouldn't be treated like chores to get through quickly. Relax the leash. Slow down so your dog can meander, scent mark (pee), and stop to sniff poles, trees, or the ground. Allow them to engage all of their senses, and they'll enjoy their outdoor time more than ever before.

PAWSITIVELY PAWSITIVE

Dog parks (or off-leash areas) are among the fastest growing kinds of parks in cities across North America. Between 2009 and 2017, the number of dog parks increased by more than 40%.

Choke collars tighten around a dog's neck when pulled

Prong collars tighten when pulled and have inwardly pointing metal spikes that dig into the skin

Shock collars deliver an electric shock to divert a dog's attention away from something or to stop an unwanted behavior

COLLARS OF CRUELTY?

Almost every companion dog wears a collar. There are all kinds of humane collars, head halters, and body harnesses that are comfortable for dogs and convenient for their guardians. But choke, prong, and shock collars should be avoided because they can cause anxiety, fear, discomfort, pain, and injury to dogs. They may cause damage to the neck, including puncture wounds, injury to the thyroid gland, windpipe (especially in short-faced dogs), esophagus, and neck vertebra. Pain, or fear of pain, causes the dog not to pull, but the dog doesn't learn what good behaviors are expected. And some dogs may become more fearful and aggressive as a result.

TOO HOT TO HANDLE!

Keeping a dog in a parked car in the summer, even if the car is in the shade with the windows cracked open, can be very dangerous. Even on mild days, a car's interior temperature can rapidly rise to 120–130° F (48.8–54°C). This can be deadly for dogs, because they don't sweat to regulate their body heat. Instead they rely on panting, but that's not enough in such a hot space. A good general rule is to never leave a dog alone in a car in the summer.

THE DOG PATROL: "HELPING ANIMALS, THOSE WITHOUT A VOICE" WITH JESSICA BROCKSOM

In November 2016, 5th grade student Jessica Brocksom learned she had been elected by her peers across the state as Connecticut's Kid Governor for the 2017 term. Her platform, *Helping Animals, Those Without A Voice*, focused on preventing animal cruelty. For the entire year, Jessica worked with the team at The Connecticut Democracy Center (CTDC), the organization who created the Kid Governor® program, to achieve her campaign goals by meeting with constituents, participating in CTDC public programs, making speeches, writing a blog, promoting collection drives in schools for animal shelters, and encouraging other students across the state to take action in promoting the humane treatment of animals. In late 2017, Jessica was also awarded the American Society for the Prevention of Cruelty to Animals' Tommy P. Monahan Kid of the Year award for her commitment to animal welfare.

Her experience as Kid Governor has made her see that kids can get involved in politics to help animals. She says, "My advice is you're never too young, start early. If you still think you're too young, start small and contact your senators or representatives and ask for some help—that's all you have to do."

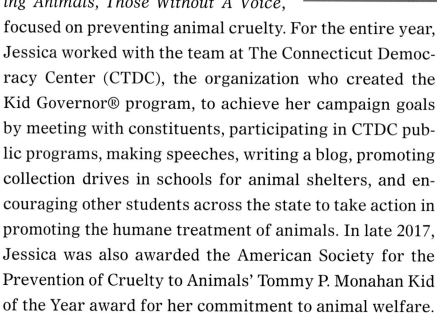

Jessica Brocksom

44

PROTECTING PRECIOUS PAWS

The salt used in winter to melt ice on sidewalks, driveways, and roads can cause discomfort or chemical burns to the paw pads of dogs. Dog shoes or boots exist to protect dog feet from salt, ice and snow. There are also special moisturizers and waxes that can be used to safeguard dog feet. It is a good idea to find walking routes that avoid heavily salted areas. And upon returning home, bare paws should be brushed and washed right away.

Walking on hot pavement in summer can be even more damaging. Pavement absorbs the sun and retains heat so it can get as hot as 120–145° F (48.8–62°C) and cause severe burns. At 125° F (51.6° C), it only takes about a minute for skin damage to occur. Artificial grass can get even hotter. Dog paws are as sensitive as human feet, so if you can't walk on it, your dog probably shouldn't either.

SENIOR DOGS ROCK!

Senior dogs have different needs than young dogs. They slow down and their fitness levels gradually decrease. Their health needs change, and age-related diseases—like arthritis, heart disease, and cancer—may surface. Senior dogs may have trouble doing things they used to do easily, such as taking long walks, jumping into a car or up onto a couch, or even just finding comfortable positions for sleep.

Extra attention should be paid to the diet of senior dogs, to ensure they're getting all the nutrients they need. Age-related issues sometimes make it difficult for shelters to adopt out senior dogs. But they can make excellent companions so if you're adding a canine member to your family consider giving a senior dog a home.

The world's oldest recorded dog was Bluey, an Australian cattle dog, who lived for 29 years and 5 months

For the largest dog breeds, like Great Danes, senior status comes early at just five to six years old

Small dogs become seniors at ten to eleven years old

If you can't feel your dog's backbone or have to press to feel the [...] your dog is pr[...] too heavy

Brooklyn Bockelmann

A dog who is shaped like a can is overweight

OVERWEIGHT DOG EPIDEMIC

Obesity (being 30% or more above ideal weight) is associated with many serious health problems, such as diabetes, liver issues, osteoarthritis and shortened lifespans. According to a 2011 survey conducted by the Association for Pet Obesity Prevention, 53% of dogs in the United States were classified as overweight or obese by their veterinarians. Dog obesity can be addressed through diet and exercise, but it's important to make sure your dog is not always hungry and miserable. To make sure you're doing the best for your dog, check with your veterinarian.

THE DOG PATROL: OPERATION O2 FUR PETS FOUNDER BROOKLYN BOCKELMANN

Le Mars, Iowa, middle school student Brooklyn Bockelmann ignited her passion for volunteering through the 4H club. But it was a Facebook page about a dog that had been rescued from a house fire using an oxygen mask that inspired her to raise the funds to buy pet masks for all of the fire and rescue services in her county. In April 2018, she started Operation O2 Fur Pets to do just that. She organized some fundraising events and set up a GoFundMe page online. Brooklyn soon had the money to accomplish her goal, but now she is thinking bigger than her own county. Since she learned that more than 40,000 pets die in fires each year, Brooklyn's new goal is provide pet oxygen masks to every one of Iowa's 600 fire departments.

When she isn't fundraising, Brooklyn also volunteers regularly at Noah's Hope Animal Rescue adoption events. She hopes to one day open a doggie daycare facility.

THE DOG PATROL: FRANCESCA JOSEPH— HARVEY'S ANIMAL HELPERS

Shortly after Hurricane Harvey forced Francesca and her family from their home in Missouri City, Texas, for five days, she saw a news report about the Humane Society of the United States rescuing dogs, cats and other animals that were left behind. Francesca immediately gathered some friends and set up a lemonade stand to raise funds for the cause. They called themselves Harvey's Animal Helpers and made a video which, along with a GoFund-Me page, helped create interest and sales in their stand, generating $3500 in a single week. Her tremendous success encouraged Francesca to raise funds and supplies for the Cleveland Amory Black Beauty Ranch, a wild animal sanctuary in Texas. It's no surprise that Francesca wants to make animal advocacy, including speaking to her elected representatives in government about animal issues, a regular part of her life. She also plans to make it her career.

Francesca Joseph

BOOMS AND BANGS ARE SCARY

Many dogs are sensitive to loud noises, including fireworks, thunder, construction equipment noise, and the loud sounds of appliances. They can make dogs anxious or fearful and cause them to shake, drool, pant, pace back and forth, hide, urinate, or vomit. Some studies suggest that slightly more than 1/5 of dogs react to loud noises, that certain breeds are more fearful than others, that female dogs are 30% more likely to be scared than male dogs, and that neutered dogs are more than 70% likely to be afraid of loud sounds than unneutered dogs. On days when you know noise might be a problem, give your dog a lot of exercise so that he's tired by the time the noise starts. Make sure he's got a safe, comfortable place to retreat indoors. Close windows and curtains or blinds to reduce the noise as much as possible.

DOG LOVER'S PLEDGE

1. I will treat all dogs with respect, compassion, and kindness.

2. I will fully satisfy the physical, psychological, and social needs of the companion dogs in my life.

3. I will spay or neuter my companion dog.

4. I will not mutilate my dog through unnecessary surgeries, such as tail docking, ear cropping, or devocalization.

5. I will never tease, neglect, abuse, or hit a dog.

6. I will only use humane, reward based, positive reinforcement training for my dog.

7. I will only adopt a dog from a shelter, pound, or rescue group.

8. I will contact a breed specific rescue group if I want to adopt a purebred dog.

9. I will not support entertainment or recreational activities that keep or use dogs in harmful ways.

10. I will speak up for dogs in my school and community.

11. I will work to establish laws that protect dogs.

12. I will support organizations that work to protect dogs.

FURTHER RESOURCES

American Society for the Prevention of Cruelty to Animals (ASPCA)
www.aspca.org

Animal Alliance of Canada (Project Jessie)
www.animalalliance.ca/projectjessie

ARTS Senior Animal Rescue
www.animalrescuetransfersociety.com

Best Friends Animal Society
bestfriends.org

Blankets Fur Beasties
www.blanketsfurbeasties.com

British Columbia SPCA
spca.bc.ca

Connecticut Public Affairs Network (Kid Governor)
kidgovernor.org

Dog Joy Books
dogjoybook.com

Dogs Deserve Better
dogsdeservebetter.org

Humane Canada
www.humanecanada.ca

Operation O2 Fur Pets
www.facebook.com/Operation O2FurPets/about

Montreal SPCA
www.spca.com/en

Moore County Citizens' Pet Responsibility Committee
mcprc.org

Northern Animal Rescue
www.northernanimalrescue.com

Sled Dogs
sleddogsfilm.com

Southern Paws
www.southernpawsinc.org

Unchain Your Dog
www.unchainyourdog.org

World Animal Protection
worldanimalprotection.ca

GLOSSARY

adaptation
the features and behaviors of an animal that help an animal survive in its natural habitat

brachycephalic
a term used to describe the abnormally short skull bone and flat face of some dog and cat breeds

breed standard
the guidelines formulated by a breed club or association that set out the attributes of each breed

bylaw
a law passed by a city or municipality

carbohydrate
sugars, starches, and fibers found in vegetables, fruit, grains, milk products, and some other foods

catch and release shelter
animal shelter that sterilizes street or stray animals, so they won't reproduce, and then sets them free in the place they were found

chaining
confining an animal to a small space by tying them up using a chain or tether

coprophagia
the eating of feces (poop)

dolichocephalic
a term that refers to animals that have relatively long skulls

domesticated
an animal that has been specifically bred for many generations to bring out particular traits that make them more suitable to living with humans

ear cropping
surgery performed on certain breeds of dogs, usually at around three months, to make their ears stand up straight rather than flop down

free-roaming dog
a dog that moves about freely and is not under the control of humans

gene
a segment of DNA that contains a code for a particular trait in a living thing

humane society
an organization for the protection and humane treatment of animals, especially those that are homeless, sick, or abused

inbreeding
the breeding of closely related animals that can concentrate disease-causing genes in the offspring and result in reduced biological fitness

Jacobson's Organ
a scent organ found in some animals that is usually located on the roof of the mouth

negative reinforcement
a training method that uses an unpleasant consequence to influence behavior

neutered
a male animal who has been sterilized so he cannot produce babies

no-kill shelter
animal shelter that aims not to kill adoptable or treatable animals, but will often not take in sick or untreatable animals

olfactory
relating to the sense of smell

omnivorous
feeding on both plant and animal foods

open admission shelter
animal shelter that provides care to both healthy, adoptable animals and sick or untreatable animals that may have to be put down

pound
a place, often run by a government agency, where stray lost, abandoned, surrendered, or seized dogs and cats are kept

positive reinforcement
a method of training that uses a pleasant or favorable reward

predator
an animal in nature that kills or preys on another animal, usually for food

puppy mill
a business that breeds puppies and focuses on maximum profit at the expense of the animals' welfare

purebred
an animal with a known, documented ancestry, bred from parents of the same breed or variety

separation anxiety
an emotional state in which dogs become upset when their guardians leave, often resulting in unwanted or destructive behaviors

socialize
to make an animal sociable and prepare him or her for human companionship

spayed
a female animal who has been sterilized so she cannot produce babies

SPCA
Society for the Prevention of Cruelty to Animals; an organization dedicated to sheltering stray animals and putting them up for adoption

sterilization
surgical removal of an animal's reproductive organs so they will not have babies

tapetum lucidum
a layer of tissue that reflects light back through the retina which enhances seeing in low light conditions

territorial
a word used to describe an animal that claims and defends a particular area as their own

tethering
confining an animal to a small space by tying them up, usually with a rope or chain

INDEX

PHOTO CREDITS